MINI
MAC

PLANES

Nicholle Carrière
& Super Explorers

What is an Airplane?

An **airplane** is a flying machine with fixed wings. An **airplane** is powered by propellers or jet engines.

Parts of an Airplane

The **cockpit** is where the pilot sits to fly the plane.

The **propeller** pulls the plane through the air.

The **ailerons** help to turn the plane.

The **landing gear**, usually wheels, lets the plane move on the ground.

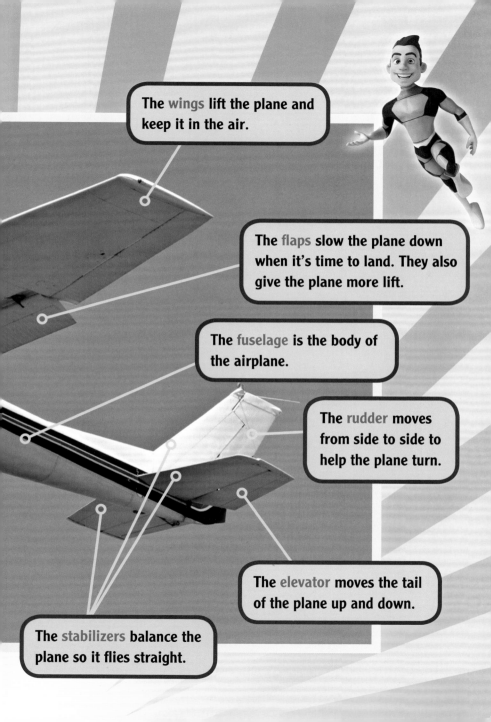

Propeller Aircraft

Propellers are only used on planes that fly slower than 770 kilometers per hour.

The first airplanes used propellers to pull them through the air. The engine turns a long metal rod called a shaft. The shaft turns the propeller.

Early propellers were made from wood. Now propellers are made from metal.

Jet Aircraft

Jets fly at about 885 kilometers per hour. That is 8 times faster than a car driving on the highway. They need to fly higher than the highest mountain. Jet planes carry passengers all over the world.

Wright Flyer (Flyer I)

The **Wright Flyer** was the first powered aircraft to fly. Brothers Orville and Wilbur Wright designed and built it. It first flew on December 17, 1903, near Kitty Hawk, North Carolina.

The plane was made of spruce wood and had a gasoline engine. Orville had to lie down to fly it.

They flew the plane four times. The longest flight was about 260 meters, or as long as two football stadiums. The flight lasted almost a minute.

Biplanes were popular until the mid-1930s. You can still see biplanes at air shows. One of the most famous biplanes was the Sopwith Camel. British pilots flew it in World War I.

Biplane

A biplane has two sets of wings. "Bi" means two. The wings are stacked one above the other. The first airplane to fly successfully, the Wright Flyer, was a biplane.

Triplane

A **triplane** has three wings stacked one on top of the other. "Tri" means three.

The Fokker Dr.I was a famous World War I triplane. It was flown by the Red Baron. Triplanes have shorter wings than biplanes. Its third wing gives a triplane better lift than a biplane.

Spirit of St. Louis

The Spirit of St. Louis was the first airplane to fly nonstop across the Atlantic Ocean. The pilot was Charles Lindbergh. Lindbergh flew the plane from New York to Paris in May 1927. The flight took 33 hours and 30 minutes.

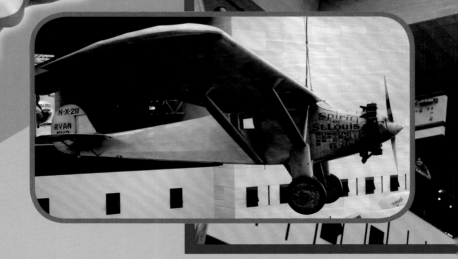

Charles Lindbergh

To make such a long flight, the plane had five fuel tanks. It had no front windshield, only two side windows. You can see the **Spirit of St. Louis** at the National Air and Space Museum in Washington, DC.

The **Cessna 172** is a small plane with one engine and four seats. It can carry a pilot and three passengers.

Cessna 172

It is a high-wing aircraft. The wings are attached to the top of the cockpit instead of to the fuselage.

The first Cessna 172 was built in 1955. More Cessna 172s have been built than any other airplane.

Ultralight

An ultralight is a small, light aircraft.
It is also called a microlight.

The smallest ultralights weigh only about 165 kilograms. That's the weight of two adult men.

Ultralights are private aircraft that people fly for fun. You can even buy a kit to build your own!

Gliders are airplanes that don't have engines. They are also called sailplanes. They have room for a pilot and one passenger.

Gliders have long, thin wings. They are towed into the air by a powered airplane then let go to fly on their own.

Glider

Gliders can fly on the air currents for five or six hours. Flying in a glider is very quiet because there is no engine. Some gliders have wheels, but most land on "skids." The skids protect the bottom of the plane and the wingtips when the glider lands.

Gossamer Albatross

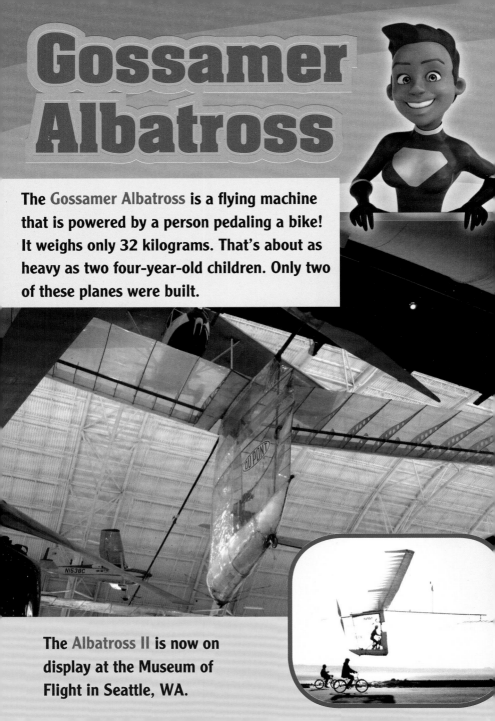

The **Gossamer Albatross** is a flying machine that is powered by a person pedaling a bike! It weighs only 32 kilograms. That's about as heavy as two four-year-old children. Only two of these planes were built.

The **Albatross II** is now on display at the Museum of Flight in Seattle, WA.

The frame is made of carbon fiber, which is light and strong. The wings and cockpit are wrapped in a kind of plastic.

It is famous for being the first human-powered airplane to fly across the English Channel on June 12, 1979. The flight was 35.6 kilometers long and lasted almost three hours. That's a long time to pedal a bike!

Floatplane

A **floatplane** is a small plane that has **floats** or **pontoons** instead of wheels.

In winter, the floats are removed, and skis can be attached. The plane can then land on ice or snow.

Floatplanes land and take off from water. They are used in places where there aren't any airports or runways. The floats make the plane heavier, so it can't fly very fast.

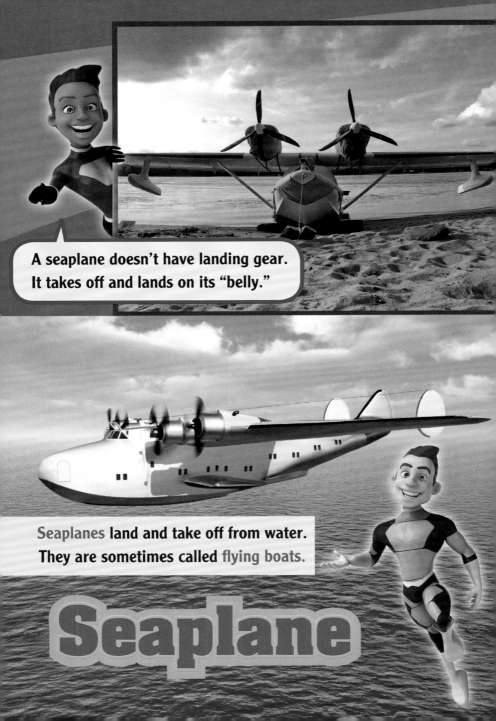

A seaplane doesn't have landing gear. It takes off and lands on its "belly."

Seaplanes land and take off from water. They are sometimes called flying boats.

Seaplane

Water Bomber

A **water bomber** is an airplane that is used for fighting fires. It has special tanks for carrying water.

The water bomber flies over a fire and drops water on the flames. It helps firefighters on the ground put out a fire.

Sometimes the tanks are filled with water when the plane is on the ground, but some water bombers can scoop up water from big lakes.

A **crop duster** is a small plane that sprays chemicals or fertilizer on farm crops. The chemicals kill bugs that eat the plants. The fertilizer helps the plants grow faster and bigger.

Crop Duster

Concorde

Concorde was a supersonic passenger jet plane. It operated from 1976 to 2003. It had four turbojet engines. Concorde could fly more than twice the speed of sound (2140 kilometers per hour). That's really fast!

The nose could drop down so pilots could see better during takeoff and landing.

Most jets take 8 hours to fly from New York to Paris. Concorde could do the trip in just 3 ½ hours!

Airbus A380

The Airbus A380 is the world's biggest passenger jet airplane. It is so big that it can only land at specially designed airports. It has two passenger decks. Most airplanes have only one. The Airbus A380 can hold 853 people!

The Airbus A380 makes the longest nonstop flights of any passenger airplane. It can fly from Houston, Texas, to Sydney, Australia, without stopping to refuel.

This is the cockpit of the Airbus A380. It's where the pilot and copilot sit to fly the plane.

Business Jet

Business jets are small and carry only a few people. They are often owned by businesses, governments or the military.

They usually have two engines on the tail or over the wings. There are more than 21,000 business jets in the world. Business jets can't travel as fast as big commercial jets.

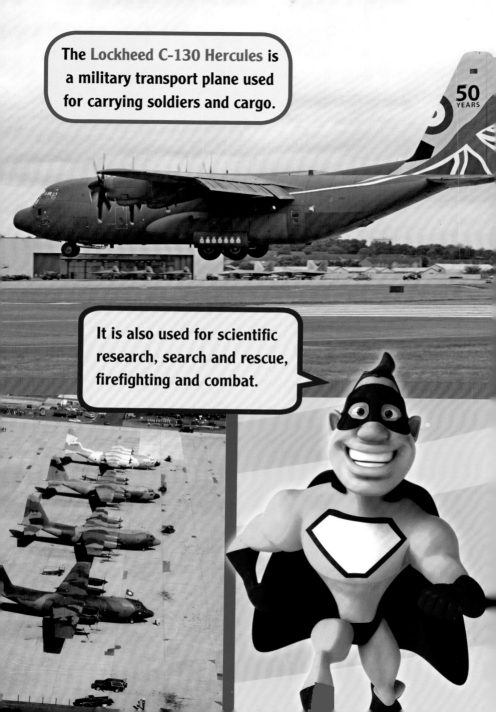

Lockheed C-130 Hercules

When the Hercules delivers supplies to bases in Antarctica, its landing gear is replaced with skis.

Airbus Beluga

The **Airbus Beluga** is one of the biggest cargo planes in the world. It's called **Beluga** because it looks like a huge white whale in the sky.

AIRBUS BELUGA 2

US BELUGA

The front of the plane can open to load and unload cargo.

The Beluga was built to carry Airbus airplane parts from the factory to where the planes are built. You need a giant airplane to carry giant airplane parts! It is also used to carry space station parts, big industrial machines and whole helicopters!

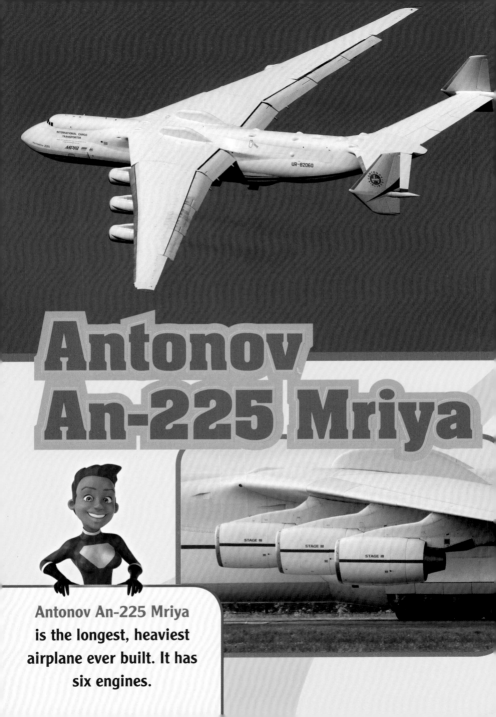

Antonov An-225 Mriya

Antonov An-225 Mriya is the longest, heaviest airplane ever built. It has six engines.

The **Antonov An-225 Mriya** is a cargo plane and holds the record for the heaviest cargo ever transported—189,980 kilograms. That's about the same weight as 32 elephants!

It has the longest wingspan of any airplane—88.4 meters—almost as long as a football field.

The landing gear has 32 wheels to support the weight of the plane and its cargo.

VTOL and V/STOL

VTOL stands for "vertical takeoff and landing." These planes can take off, land and hover vertically (standing up). They don't need a runway.

V/STOL stands for "vertical or short takeoff and landing." These planes take off and land either vertically or from a short runway.

Stealth aircraft are used by the military. They are called "stealth" because they are hard to see on radar.

These planes can carry a pilot but no passengers.

They have special shapes and often look flattened. The outside of the plane absorbs radar so radar can't "see" the plane.

Stealth Aircraft

The **SR-71 Blackbird** is a United States Air Force plane. It holds the record for being the fastest jet aircraft.

It set the speed record of 3530 kilometers per hour on July 28, 1976.

The **SR-71 Blackbird** flew with a crew of two, a pilot in front and an officer to do surveillance behind the pilot. The plane was named "Blackbird" because of its dark color.

SR-71 Blackbird

Drones

870

Nowadays anyone can buy a small drone to fly remotely for work or fun. Drones can have video cameras to see the ground from above. Small drones can even be used to deliver packages.

A drone is an unmanned aircraft. That means it doesn't need a pilot. It flies by remote control. Drones carry cameras and many different kinds of sensors. Some can read a car's license plate from more than 3 kilometers away. That's almost 40 city blocks!

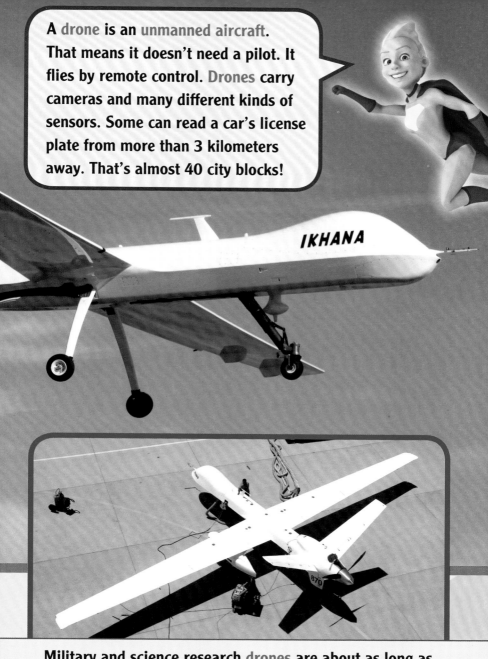

IKHANA

Military and science research drones are about as long as a school bus. Their wingspan is longer than a train boxcar.

Shuttle Carriers are special Boeing 747s that carried space shuttles from the landing area at the Kennedy Space Center in Florida to other landing or takeoff sites.

United States

Shuttle Carrier Aircraft

SpaceShipOne

SpaceShipOne was a rocket-powered plane. It looked like an airplane, but it had a rocket engine. Only three people could ride in it—a pilot and two passengers.

SpaceShipOne couldn't take off by itself. A special airplane called White Knight carried it high into the air and then let it go.

Most passenger jets can fly at about 12,000 meters (12 kilometers) off the ground. SpaceShipOne flew at 112,000 meters (112 kilometers). It could fly in space above Earth's atmosphere!

North American X-15

The North American X-15 could also fly higher than any jet airplane. It reached an altitude of 108,000 meters (108 kilometers).

Because it traveled so fast, the outside of the plane got very hot. It was made of a special high-strength metal that could withstand high temperatures.

Air Racing

In **air racing**, small planes fly around an obstacle course.

The planes have to fly around and between tall cones called "pylons." The pylons are full of air and tear if a plane hits them. Racing planes are small and have only one seat. The wings are short, so the planes can move fast and turn quickly.

Pilots get penalties for flying too high, hitting pylons or not doing the course correctly. The winner is the plane with the fastest time and the fewest penalties.

In aerobatics, planes do tricks like loops, rolls, spins and stalls. It is also called stunt flying. Aerobatics are popular at air shows. Sometimes the planes leave a smoke trail so that people watching can see the tricks better.

Pilots who do aerobatics have to be very good. It is difficult to do all the fancy tricks safely.

Aerobatics

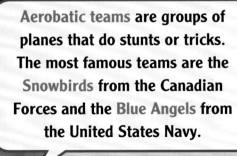

Aerobatic teams are groups of planes that do stunts or tricks. The most famous teams are the Snowbirds from the Canadian Forces and the Blue Angels from the United States Navy.

First printed in 2017 10 9 8 7 6 5 4 3 2 1

Printed in China

The Publisher: Mega Machines is an imprint of Blue Bike Books

Library and Archives Canada Cataloguing in Publication

Carrière, Nicholle, 1961–, author
Planes / Nicholle Carrière.
(Super explorers)
Issued in print and electronic formats.

ISBN 978-1-926700-74-8 (softcover)
ISBN 978-1-926700-75-5 (epub)

1. Airplanes—Juvenile literature. I. Title.

TL547.C33 2017   j629.133'34   C2017-901926-0   C2017-901927-9

Frontcover: SR-71 Blackbird,Judson Brohmer USAF/Public domain; background image, Stavklem/Thinkstock

Backcover: Biplane Sopwith Camel, USAF/Public domain; Concorde, Eduard Marmet/CC BY-SA 3-0; VTOL Harrier, Mate 3rd Class Andrew King, US Navy/Public domain-Wiki

Photo Credits: 350z33 16-17; Ad Meskens 16; Adrian Pingstone 8a, 18, 19ab, 21ab, 44a, 63a; aeroprints-com 41; Ahrys_Art/Thinkstock 8b; Alan Radecki 30; Alan Wilson 12; Alex; Beltyukov 42a; Alexskiba/Thinkstock 2, 6-7; Apisorn/Thinkstock 57b; Argestes/Thinkstock 23; ASafaric/Thinkstock 31b; Avitya 62; bomberpilot 38; ChrisBoswell 7; Christian Kath 34-35; Cory Denton 63c; D Ramey Logan 56-57, 58, 61a; dan_prat/Thinkstock 48b; dell640/ Thinkstock 2-3; Dhaluza 22a; Dllu 27; Dmitry A Motti 42b; Eduard Marmet 34; Emdx 26; Hgrobe 45a; icholakov/ Thinkstock 14; IMNATURE/Thinkstock 40; iv-serg; Thinkstock 28a; JetRequest_com 39b; Jon Sullivan 63d; Jupiterimages/Thinkstock 26-27; kot63/Thinkstock 20-21; laurendiscipio/Thinkstock 22b; Laurent ERRERA 40-41; lbraceland/Thinkstock 4-5; MatthiasKabel 63b; MR1805/Thinkstock 28b, 29; Murmakova/Thinkstock 6; Mustang_Renato Spilimberg Carvalho 39a; Naddsy 37; NASA 24b, 25, 54-55, 55, 59ab; nikename/Thinkstock 8-9; Oleg Belyakov 31a; Philip Lange/Thinkstock 46-47; Ryan Somma 24a; RyanKing999/Thinkstock 52; Senohrabek/ Thinkstock 36-37; Sergey Khantsis 43b; Sitikka/Thinkstock 15; Stefan Krause 32-33; Steve Fitzgerald 35; Stocktrek Images/Thinkstock 52-53, 53; tataquax 60; Tony Hisgett 61b; US Navy 47; USAF 13, 44b, 45b, 48a, 49, 50ab, 51; USDA 32; USDOD 46; Vasiliy Koba 43a; Vipre77/Thinkstock 57a.

Background Graphics: IgorZakowski/Thinkstock 8,-9, 10-11, 14-15, 24-25, 28-29, 38-39, 50-51, 58-59; iwanara-MC/Thinkstock 32-33, 36-37, 56-57, 62-63; shelma1/Thinkstock 4-5, 54-55, 60-61.

Superhero Illustrations: julos/Thinkstock.

Produced with the assistance of the Government of Alberta, Alberta Media Fund.

We acknowledge the financial support of the Government of Canada.

Funded by the Government of Canada
Financé par le gouvernement du Canada | Canada

PC: 28